How to Let Go of Your Mad Baggage

.

How to Let Go of Your Mad Baggage

Lynne Namka, Ed. D.

Illustrated by Nancy Sarama

Talk, Trust and Feel Therapeutics

TUCSON, ARIZONA

Also by Lynne Namka

The Doormat Syndrome, Health Communications, 1989.

The Mad Family Gets Their Mads Out: Fifty Things Families Can Say and Do to Express Anger Constructively, Talk, Trust and Feel Therapeutics, 1995.

Published by
Talk, Trust and Feel Therapeutics
5398 Golder Ranch Road
Tucson, Arizona 85737

Designed and produced by Harrison Shaffer / Whitewing Press

Printed in the United States of America

10   9   8   7   6   5   4   3   2   1

Library of Congress Catalog Card Number 95-62300

ISBN 0-9642167-1-X

Dedication

This book is dedicated to the three neat Human Beings for whom it is my privilege to be mother—John M. Grimes, Kathy Sbarboro, and Karen Armstrong—and to my dear husband, Gordon Harnack, who is learning about his mads.

How to Let Go of Your Mad Baggage

It is through having experienced all experience that the soul finally achieves perfect sympathy and understanding.

—JOSEPH CAMPBELL

Life is a schoolhouse.
 We Human Beings are the pupils.
 We are here to learn about our feelings
 For Human Beings are curious beings.
 This is the Great Human Drama
 Where Human Beings learn to balance their emotions
 And look at distorted beliefs that cause upset feelings.
 Everyday experiences of Life's Drama present a personal curriculum.
 Our emotions provide us with opportunities for understanding and growth,
 For feelings are to be experienced and expressed so that we can evolve.
 All we need to do is sign up for the course work
 So that we can get to be a real, grown-up Human Being
 Who understands that "To feel is to heal."
 Whether or not to enroll in this curriculum is your choice.
 One great thing about being a Human Being is that you do get choices.

What are these things called mads?
>Mads are feeling of anger we have
When someone hurts, opposes, offends or annoys us.
For Human Beings are emotional beings.
The Human Condition is for people to have mads.
Everyone has mads.
Big people, little people,
Even deeply spiritual people have mads.
All colors and cultures of people have mads.
We have mads because we are human.
All Human Beings can have angry feelings
When someone or something threatens us.
A Human Being is a very lovely thing to be even if we do have mads.

Mads come in all sizes and shapes.
>Some people have little mads.
Some people have big mads.
Some people's mads have a long fuse
That takes a long time for them to get angry.
Other people's mads have a short fuse.
When people blow their fuse often, it's called quick temper.
When they bombard others with their mads, it's called rage.
Short fuse or long fuse, the mads turn ordinary people into
Red-hot firecrackers or time bombs ready to explode.

Mads come about when Human Beings feel hurt or bad inside.
  Mads are feelings we have when someone or something threatens:
  Our bodies,
  Our possessions,
  Our self-esteem,
  Our values,
  Our not getting what we think we deserve,
  Or when someone trespasses on our sense of justice and fair play.
  Anger is one response Human Beings can make when they are
  threatened.

Anger is an energy that comes up very quickly
  For we Human Beings are energy beings
  Whose mads flare up when our personal space is violated.
  Mads happen when Human Beings are provoked.
  They come when we are threatened and feel bad inside.
  They pop out when we insist that ours is the only way of doing things.
  They can happen when we tell ourselves, "It's not fair."
  Anger is one of the feelings we can have when we don't get our way.
  The mads are one way that Human Beings deal with hurt and pain.

Anger is a heavy emotion that can get stuck and weigh us down.
    Mads are sometimes carried around for years and years
    Stored in stiff necks, hurting backs and jittery stomachs.
    Mads cause us to have monkey chatter brains and circular thinking.
    They breed in our central nervous system.
    They wreak havoc in our bodies.
    Human Beings do not like having mads.
    In fact, they hate having mads
    And do all manner of things to keep from feeling their pain.
    So to avoid their mads, some people become little robots
    Going through the motions of life with frozen feelings.
    Some people actually deny that they have bad feelings.
    Others try to get rid of their mads by throwing them out on others.
    One of the hardest things about being a Human Being is to have mads.

Some Human Beings come down with a big case of the mads
    And some people have a ***Big, Heavy Case Of The Mads.***
    They lug their case of mads around all the time.
    Besides their mads suitcase, they wear backpacks
    Filled with hurt, fear, guilt and shame.
    Human Beings become pack rats of their own negative emotions.
    Some try to run away from their uncomfortable feelings
    But those backpacks and cases of mads go right with them.

Yes, Human Beings do have mads all right.

    Those pesky mads.

    They keep us stewing and steaming.

    They make us irrational.

    They pop out at the wrong time.

    They make us do and say things we regret later.

    They cause our tummy to feel yucky inside.

    All Human Beings have some kind of mads.

    It's okay to have mads if you are firm and fair about it.

    It is what you do with your mads that count.

    The more you know about your mads, the wiser you will be.

    Wise, wise Human Beings have worked through numerous mads.

    Just remember, having mads is human and that is a marvelous thing to be.

JUST WHO IS THE TEACHER HERE?

The mads curriculum is all around you.

    Just as there are many students, there are many teachers.

    Look about you:

    Many courses about your mads are available.

    When the student is ready, the teacher will come.

    Teachers come in all manner of unusual shapes and sizes.

    People and things that anger us can be seen as opportunities for growth.

    Watch out!

    That angry person with whom you are having so much trouble

    Just may be your teacher giving you the opportunity to look at yourself.

For Human Beings, life is meant to be enjoyed.
  This marvelous universe is meant to be savored.
  You are here to learn to have healthy relationships with others
  And to live lightly on our planet.
  To do so, you need to check out that backpack and suitcase.
  Balancing the emotions is one of the tasks that Human Beings face.
  The goal of the mads curriculum is to learn to love yourself and others.
  The grades you receive will be reflected in the quality of your life.
  Growth is optional,
  But highly recommended.

Choices. It is about choices.
  Life is about choices.
  We don't have to keep doing the same-o, same-o.
  We can learn to choose safe ways to take care of our mads.
  We members of the Great Human Tribe can be very, very choicy
  When it comes to expressing our mads.
  Choose wisely.

Sign up for the Courses
Show up for Classes
Do The Homework
Learn the Lessons
Day by day Pop
Quizzes will be
Given

How the Mads Come to Be

Everyone is doing the best he or she can under the circumstances. If you don't understand how they could do this, then you don't understand their circumstances.

—Virginia Satir

One of the most challenging things about life is being in relationships.
    For Human Beings are social beings
    Who use their relationships to learn about
    Their disruptive feelings, thoughts, beliefs and behavior.
    Now all interactions of Human Beings are energy trades.
    Each person has a reservoir of energy stored in his or her batteries
    Which get drained and recharged through dealings with others.
    A person's battery or vital life force expands and contracts
    Depending on the quality of their interactions in relationships.
    Equality between people produces a reciprocal exchange.
    Respect, acceptance and openness create balanced energy.
    Manipulation and domination drain the juice out of human batteries.
    Human Beings have this unusual system of battery charging:
    Families are the place where most Human Beings
    Learn about the pain of getting their batteries jumped.

Each family has its own unique mad traditions.
  Most families equate "bad" with mads.
  The problem is that most families do not know how to discuss conflict.
  Some parents believe they can open up their own case of the mads,
  But they tell the children not to feel bad, cry or get angry.
  "Do as I say, not as I do" is a message that confuses the little ones,
  For most adults have strong feelings of anger.
  Children soak up their parents' anger energy.
  Some children's batteries become drained,
  Other children's batteries get highly charged with anger.
  The little ones feel bad. They cry. They get angry.
  They learn it is bad to have uncomfortable feelings.
  Then to be safe, they have to hide their bad feelings.
  They are little Human Beings after all.

THE MAD FAMILY GOES WEST

Little Human Beings who have been hurt learn about hurt.
Hurt is an energy that must find a place to go.
Punishing and shaming cause little ones to experience great pain
And fill up their suitcases and backpacks.
Children take on their parents' messages of "mad equals bad."
When they are told not to get angry or have disagreeable feelings,
Little Human Beings come down with a case of the bads
That could stick around for their entire life.
Children learn their parents' angry ways of dealing with threat
And take their backpacks and cases of mads
To the playground, to the schools, and to the streets.
Grown-up children pass the family mads on to the next generation.
From one group to another—
Mads here, mads there, mads spread everywhere.
Mads are passed around from one Human Being to the other.

Some parenting styles give children large cases of mads and bads.
    Some parents have a "Too Cold, Too Busy and Don't Give Enough" style.
    Neglect creates a child with a poor base of security in the world.
    A child who does not experience love and caring becomes secretly angry.
    Some parents are the "Too Hot, You Can't Do Anything Right" type.
    Constant criticism produces a child who beats up self and others.
    Then there is the "Pushover, Give Too Much" style of parent.
    These children demand that the world give them everything,
    And of course it doesn't, so they feel justified in being angry.

There is the "Too Fearful, Be Careful, You Will Get Hurt" parent.
    Insecurity produces angry children afraid to risk
    Who are afraid to know, show or even feel their mads.
    And the "Too Controlling, What Will People Think?" kind of parent.
    Dominated children give up themselves to meet others' needs,
    And are angry that they have to be someone they are not.
    The "Come Here—Go Away, Yes You Can—No You Can't" parent
    Creates a child who is confused by the conflicting double messages.
    These little ones become immobile with no sense of direction,
    And when they finally figure this out, they are really angry.
    Then there is the "I Have the Right to Hit or Hurt Your Body" parent.
    Abusive parents create children who go through life frightened and angry,
    Who hide out from the world or repeat those same hurtful acts on others.

18

Blaming and shaming ways of parents produce hurt and angry children
  Whose life force and energy resources become distorted.
  Criticized children become angry. Spoiled children become angry.
  Abandoned children become very angry.
  Neglected children become very angry.
  Children who have been abused become very, very angry.
  Too much or too little, too strong, or too weak, too hot or too cold—
  Little children suffer the too-much or too-little actions of their parents.

Now this is not to blame parents for this sorry state of human nature
  For parents often do to their children what was done to them.
  Unresolved pain of the parent comes out in excesses and deficits
  of behavior.
  Human Beings generally act in ways learned from their parents.
  Which was learned from their parents. So back in time it goes
  For Human Beings are interdependent beings.
  The baggage of aggression and dominance can be traced back through
  the generations.
  The pain of the parents is visited on their offspring.
  Angry Human Beings are victims of victims of victims.

Some Human Beings in this generation are trying to be different
  For Human Beings are caring beings
  Who are learning about aggressive, negative energy
  And about the cost of the baggage of those mads and bads.
  Today many parents look for new ways to interact with their children.
  Some have learned to charge their own batteries
  So they don't need to take energy from others.
  Some parents are changing what they didn't like in their own upbringing,
  Choosing to raise their own children gently and lovingly
  Allowing a free exchange and flow of energy between all concerned.
  Some families are finding healthy ways to express their anger.
  Many parents today are deciding to sign up for the mads courses.
  Then they can be a "family of glads" instead of the mads and bads.
  Hopefully, the Great Human Tribe is slowly starting to change.

Courses You Can Take to Learn about Your Mads

To know all is to understand all and this leaves no room for judgment and condemnation.
—CLARENCE DARROW

The mads curriculum can be exceedingly complex
    For Human Beings are complicated beings
    Who are given the opportunity to understand themselves and others,
    And study the numerous forms that angry energy takes.
    Warning: The contents of the mads course work may take a lifetime.
    Working out anger is no easy task for a Human Being.
    But the mads curriculum can be a necessary and satisfying challenge
    Especially for those who want to be mature grown-up people.
    Life allows continual registration and enrollment,
    Day-by-day pop quizzes will be given.

At times, anger energy hovers heavily in the air waiting to be caught
    For Human Beings are susceptible beings,
    Who are capable of taking in other people's anger.
    The contagion of anger is as catching as the latest virus.
    Certain trigger words, gestures or inflammatory ideas push our buttons.
    Instant-replay anger buttons are easily activated when we are stressed.
    Automatic anger flares up more frequently when body resources are low.
    Other people's mads are like a piece looking for a fit in a jigsaw puzzle.
    Free floating anger searches for receptor hooks in other people to latch onto.
    But it doesn't come in if there is no negative association with that issue.
    The mads curriculum warns you about picking up additional anger
    As you empty out the junk in your backpack and suitcase.
    Enroll in the mads course work and get inoculated for the anger virus
    And learn to clear out your own anger receptor sites.
    Bonus for curriculum completion:
    A working knowledge of your red flags and "Settle Down Button."

So get yourself down to the vaccination place and get yourself a booster shot for that human virus called the mads. Then take the course **Keeping Other People's Mads Out of Your Own Baggage.**

Anger is a heavy, pulling, invasive energy
  For Human Beings are magnetic beings
  Whose angry thoughts produce angry emotions.
  Angry emotions translate into angry behavior.
  Feelings, thoughts, beliefs and behavior translate into experience.
  Feelings, thoughts, beliefs and behavior *cause* all experience.
  Angry people often are biased toward seeing nebulous situations as
  hostile.
  Those prone to vent their anger easily get even angrier.
  Hostility follows hostility. Anger begets more anger.
  Angry energy always follows angry thought.
  Continuous angry thoughts can cause a reality of crisis and bad luck.

Underneath anger is a frequency of fear
  For Human Beings are fearful beings
  Who substitute anger for the remembrance of having been hurt in the past.
  Fear is the energy of lack and being unworthy.
  It is the pain of loss sadly resulting in an inability to trust.
  The fear frequency can tune in at the conscious level
  Or it can hide underground mucking around in the subconscious.
  Fear causes us to jump out of the present, back into the past
  Into those same old ways we felt as children.
  The fear vibration drains our batteries.
  Some Human Beings substitute anger to avoid their frequency of fear.

An archaeological course to take might be titled **Digging Up the Past: Getting to the Roots of Your Anger.**

We live in angry times.
    The horror of anger run rampant takes many disguises.
    For Human Beings are aggressive beings
    With greed, hatred and ignorance as part of their fabric.
    Bullying and intimidation are basic tools of coercion.
    Ridicule and put-downs are used to try to keep others in line.
    Racial, sexual orientation and cultural humor are more subtle forms of
    anger.
    Shaming and blaming are often used to try to silence others.
    Aggressive, dominant anger energy rips and penetrates the essence of
    others.
    Taken to the extreme, anger maims, destroys and kills.
    Human Beings can become flamed by the negative energies of anger.

Many channels of fear exist to keep people caught in arousal
    For Human Beings are sensation-seeking beings.
    Inflammatory words can give others the sanction to violence.
    The channels of fear and anger beget more fear and anger
    Causing some frightened Human Beings to act out their mads.
    Daily observation of aggression can cause more hostility.
    Continuous anger thoughts can turn into aggressive behavior.
    Angry energy intensified turns into bigotry and hate.
    When human rights are violated, further anger breaks out.
    At times the fear energy sparks into spontaneous combustion.
    On a small scale, angry combustion is called violence.
    On a large scale, combative anger is called war.
    Human Beings would do well to look good and hard at the spread of mads.

Search out the influences that promote anger. Then take the course
called **Modern Day Culture and the Forms of Anger Unleashed in
the World.**

Anger that is rationalized and justified can become compulsive
   For Human Beings are addictive beings
   Who can use their mads to create great dramas
   And spice up an altogether too-boring life.
   Some people become addicted to the energy of anger.
   Some have high thresholds of excitability and low thresholds of
   frustration.
   Their drug of choice is self-manufactured to mask the emptiness inside.
   To feel alive, some angry people need the adrenaline fix and power surge
   That accompanies controlling or hurting others.
   They use their anger to leech the life force energy of others.
   Mads that run amok can take over a person's life so that
   They become prisoners of their own hormones and central nervous
   system.
   One choice Human Beings can make is to change their perception.
   With attitudinal shifts, Human Beings can switch over to a new channel.

Those who want to break the anger/addiction cycle and return to their true self might try the self-help group **AAA: Adrenaline Addiction Anonymous.**

Nice People Do Get Angry

How often the angry man rages denial of what his inner self is telling him.

—FRANK HERBERT

Nice people have mads.
    Even very nice people have mads.
    "White hat" people are terrified of confrontations with others
    And afraid of knowing or showing their own anger.
    They want to be known as the good guys and gals who are the peacemakers,
    So they stuff their upsets and irritable emotions
    And camouflage themselves in a coat of many colors.
    White hat people's insides don't match their outsides,
    But sooner or later, those seething mads have their say.
    Remember, angry energy has to have a place to go.
    Sometimes the mads seep out in cold rage.
    Other times they explode out with the last straw with the
    Illusion of the white hat and many-colored coat blown to smithereens.

Some people say they never get angry with others.
    They get upset. Or stressed.
    Or bummed out. Or irritated.
    Worst case scenario, they are frustrated. But not angry.
    They've been programmed to follow the old family script—
    "Don't get mad."
    So, being loyal to their old programming, they don't.
    They won't. They can't.
    Mom and Dad said "It Is Just Not Allowed. Don't Do Mads!"
    Following Mom and Dad's old rules gives an illusion of safety.
    Guilt about breaking old family rules keeps change from happening.
    White hat people could focus on denial of their negative human emotions
    And the contents of that backpack and suitcase they carry with them.

People who disavow their anger have an ongoing pilot light.
> They are so afraid of being rejected that they stifle their irritations.
> Being so desperately dependent upon the people they love,
> They have to stuff their mads because it's not safe.
> They have the fear belief of,
> "If I let the people I love know how angry I am, they will leave me."
> Overly dependent people can't voice or know the depth of their pain.
> Often they turn it inward where it leads to helplessness and despair.
> Depression can harbor the belief of "What's the point of being angry?
> No one will listen to me anyway. There is no point."
> Not having a say so, even to one's self causes an eventual energy shortage.
> That simmering pilot light of disavowed anger burns away, using up vitality.

The course to take to release shut down feelings is **Letting It All Out and Living Your Life as a Real Person with Honest-to-Goodness Feelings.**

Some angry Human Beings beat themselves up on a regular basis.
    They are "anger-inners" calling themselves
    Handy names to acknowledge what a goof up they really are.
    "Anger inners" always have a convenient target handy.
    Their own "should monsters" lurks inside saying what bad people
    they are.
    Their "shoulds" run their lives pointing out all imperfections,
    While their immune system listens and responds in kind.
    Angry energy turned back on the self devastates body and mind.
    Negative self-talk destroys one's sense of well-being.
    Less-than-perfect people could learn to cut themselves some slack
    And allow themselves to be real Human Beings, warts and all.

Bodies know when fear beliefs and negative scripts shut down feelings
    For Human Beings are also physical beings whose
    Unexpressed anger lurks around the body poking at vital parts.
    Vital parts understand that anger is a most human emotion,
    And should be expressed rather than squelched.
    Shut down people's lives get caught in the cycle of:
    "Don't be angry. I am angry—I'm not allowed to feel it."
    Distorted feelings produce intense physical reactions.
    Bodies become ill from all that pretending.
    To keep from storing unnecessary anger,

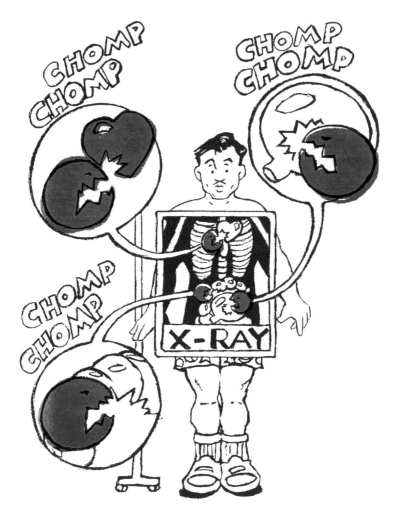

Mads should be experienced for what they are:
Pent up, uncomfortable energy seeking expression.
Denied anger increases in shape and size, becoming stagnant energy.
If they are not released mads can turn into body dis-ease.
Sickness can be a way of the body's trying to purge negative energy.
Hospitals are full of people who believe that they should not get angry.
Vital parts do not like holding onto negative energies.
Human Beings would do well to remember that "Feeling is healing."

Maybe people who don't acknowledge their anger could take the course called **Letting Your Outsides Match Your Insides: Real People Do Get Mad and Can Own It and Show It.**

The power of healing lies in feeling and acknowledging the feelings.
The power of healing lies in the word.
Whether in thought or spoken aloud,
Affirming words are powerful tools for change.
Anger inners are given numerous opportunities to make mistakes
And observe how their negative self-talk only makes matters worse.
That "should monster" that hides inside can be softened to choices
and preferences.
Repressed anger can be let out so it doesn't manifest as illness.
What to say to oneself after goofing up royally
Is one of those great opportunities that Human Beings get to make.

The public speaking course on positive affirmations to take is **Change Your Words, Change Your Life!**

THE BIG GAME OF LIFE

The Not-So-Nice Guys and Gals

An angry man is full of poison.
—CONFUCIUS

Underneath impassioned, angry struggles are the real issues.
Human Beings rarely fight about what they fight about
For Human Beings are controlling beings
Whose "should monster" likes to say "You should . . . "
The real issue of a confrontation often revolves around
Who is in charge and who has
The right to make up the other person's mind.
And how much anger and force is needed to make the other person change?

Needing to be in control of other people is "The Big Game of Life."
"The Big Game of Life" is "I have the right to tell you what to do!"
The rules of The Big Game insist:
"I have the right to decide how you should change.
And I have the right to dominate you and get my way."
The bottom line in The Big Game is control and power.
People who play this contest feel good about getting their way over others.
People who participate in The Big Game may win some of their battles,
But they lose the war and often end up lonely and bitter.

People who are trying to give up The Big Game of Life could take the course called **Giving Up the Need to Be Number One All of the Time.**

Some people's Big Game takes the form of "withholds" and "stonewalling."
    Some parents withhold attention or love when they are angry.
    So the children, in turn, learn to pout, refuse to talk and glare.
    "Withholders" say *"I'll show you how mad I am by not talking to you."*
    "Stonewallers" deny the problem and refuse to deal with it.
    Their life becomes a series of guards and walls set up for self-protection.
    Keeping the guards up requires so much personal energy that
    They end up shutting out those very ones they love.
    "Withholders" and "stonewallers" have hired their guards so long ago that
    They don't know that their guards are still on the payroll.

Some angry Human Beings delight in holding grudges and using paybacks.
    Grudges are revving up the old hurts to justify remaining angry.
    Paybacks are revenge ideas or behaviors that hurt others.
    While thinking *"I feel good scheming about how I can hurt you."*
    Spiteful people concentrate on their own injustice and miss the bigger picture.
    Withholds, grudges and paybacks block the free flow of energy between people.
    People who play the Big Game of retaliation could use some belief busting.
    As the old saying goes, "Success is always the best revenge."
    So when life in all its various forms hands out bumps and betrayals,
    The choice can become whether to be bitter or better.

The life saving course to take here is **How to Let Go of Revenge and Reclaim Your Mind** subtitled **I'm Not Giving Revenge Thoughts Free Rent in My Brain Anymore.**

The assigned term paper to write for this course is called **There Ain't No Bad Guy—There Is Only Problem Solving.**

People who play The Big Game may use below-the-belt fighting,
   Which always guarantees that the problem will not get worked out.
   Dirty fighting is triggered by old, unresolved childhood
   Hurts and unhealthy ways of coping with threat.
   Withdrawal, sarcasm, attacking and denying that a problem exists
   Always turn up the heat and feed the fire in an argument.
   No one ever gets what he or she wants by calling other people names.
   Piggybacking of old problems sidetracks the issue being discussed.
   When emotional arousal gets too high, reason runs right out the window.
   In below-the-belt fighting, neither person ever really wins.

Some couples engage in The Big Game of crazy-making behaviors where
   Provocation, accusations and counterattack are the daily fare.
   Both partners harbor unrealistic expectations that trigger further
   alienation,
   Which keeps the vicious blaming and discounting cycle going.
   A's angry behavior leads to B's angry behavior
   Which further escalates the hostility.
   And so on it goes, each pulling in and pushing each other away,
   Each backing the other into a lonely corner of stubbornness and betrayal.
   Unforgivable resentments can build up, creating an impasse.
   The "Let's fight and make up" pattern causes a swirling energy of chaos.

Do Fight, But Fight Fair is the course to take for those who goad their
partner on to the point of continual hurt and hostility.

On an energetic level, out-of-control, combative anger between people
Is a negative feedback loop that
Bounces back and forth from one person to another.
It thrusts and penetrates the energy fields of the other.
Mean-spirited anger is manipulative and dehumanizing
That tries to win at all costs.
With each person flame throwing against each other saying,
"I'll show you how tough I can be.
I'll hurt you before you hurt me.
I can say and do more harmful things than you.
Don't come too close or you're really going to get it."
Combative anger keeps the couple sandblasting each other,
Causing a sad deterioration of the relationship and the sense of self.
Human Beings can learn to break into that destructive feedback loop
And balance their dual needs for connection and independence.

There is an unhealthy bonding when people are caught in a Sticky Putty
relationship
Where the violent energies of submission/dominance coexist
With pulling and stretching of the adhesive threads
That bind and hold the couple stuck together.
Seething energy ricochets between the two people
And snaps back and forth like a taut rubber band.
Couples who engage in destructive submissive/dominance energies
Are desperate because they can't live together but can't live apart.
Freedom from this detrimental type of relationship
Can only be achieved by much introspection, personal growth and
The blessing and severing of those Sticky Putty threads.

If your fights with your loved ones are long and vicious, you can get help
at the workshop called **How to Break Out of Angering Yourself and
Others.**

Some Human Beings have the mistaken idea that their world must be perfect.

They overinvest in themselves, believing that they are special
And they expect others to make everything right for them.
Unable to acknowledge their own personal shortcomings,
They project their unmet needs for power on others.
These people are "anger outers" throwing their demands about,
For some Human Beings can be dramatic beings
Whose anger is often irrational and impulsive.
They shoot from the hip when feeling insulted or injured,
"Stick 'em up or I'll shoot. I'm the chosen one here.
You owe me. Give me what I want or I'll explode,
Or I'll withdraw my love from you!"
But no matter how much "anger outers" get, it is never enough.
They have a big hole inside that can't be filled by their demands on others.

Some people become "takers," feeling entitled to trash the needs of others
Insisting on power and compliance from those around them.
Anger that holds a demand hook can be exploitative.
"Takers" feel good about getting their own way.
Gaining self-esteem when using others is
An elaborate cover-up for denying one's own pain.
Having a great empty vacuum inside,
"Takers" need to obtain their energy from other people.
But of course they can't be concerned about how others are depleted.
Sadly, "takers" never learn some of the most exquisite attributes of Human Beings:
Empathy, compassion and walking a mile in the other person's moccasins.

Courses for Takers are scarce. **Highly recommended is deep introspection to recognize and combat that "You owe me" outlook on life.**

But "takers" can't be "takers" unless they hook up with "givers,"
Who have their own skewed needs of giving in to the demands of others.
"Givers" appoint themselves the role of the keeper of the relationship,
And see themselves as being the Elmer's glue of the family.
They give to others what has not been given to themselves
In hopes that the good things of life will be granted to them.
"Givers" often harbor secret hurt and anger over not being appreciated
For all the hard work they have assigned themselves.
Underneath excessive giving can lie the hidden need to control others.
If you listen carefully you might hear the great sucking sound
When givers allow takers to drain their batteries in the name of love.
The contract to give too much can result in intense negative feelings
And an unfulfilled life that ends up as an angry martyr/victim.
Givers and takers, inners and outers, too much or too little.
It all boils down to the form that the Human Being's life takes.

Givers could sign up for a self help group called **Standing Up For Ourselves-Doormats No More.**

Some people use "bully behavior" to express their anger.
　　They are "anger outers" who tease, threaten and intimidate others.
　　"Anger outers" expand out their energy walls to show their power.
　　They foster beliefs of deserving everything they can get
　　And feel justified in using cruelty and violence to get it.
　　They don't honor the rights of other people to be safe
　　And go to great lengths to rationalize their hurtful ways.
　　No matter how it's rationalized, hurting others is always bully behavior.
　　The energies of hot air intimidation are used as a tactic
　　To puff ones' self up to try to prevent loss of personal control.
　　"Anger outers" may sometimes get their way in the short run,
　　But they miss that deep sense of self satisfaction
　　That the fine art of negotiation and compromise can bring.

Perhaps takers and people with bully behavior missed the kindergarten course on **How to Take No for an Answer and Still Feel Good about Yourself.**

And the elementary school courses on **Give Up the "You Owe Me" Attitude** and **Letting Go of Intimidation for Fun and Profit.**

Human Beings do strange things to dodge their uncomfortable feelings,
    For some Human Beings are avoidant beings
    Who have ways to sidestep feeling susceptible and exposed.
    Some people turn to alcohol and drugs to medicate their pain.
    Others who can't access their emotions are called "repressors."
    They must keep their energy constricted and their body numbed.
    "Repressors" have a fear of being emotionally out of control
    And deep embedded scripts of not becoming exposed or vulnerable.
    At times, they may venture forth to express their bad feelings,
    Then get frightened and refuse to claim any uncomfortable emotions.
    "Repressors" bounce into the experience of being real and feeling,
    Then back out of sync with their true sense of self.
    They sleepwalk through life trying to avoid feelings of unworthiness,
    Lashing out at others occasionally to try to feel alive.
    Frozen feelings help keep their robot in charge.
    So they never get "busted" about squashing their pain.

Some angry people become fugitives, running from their own pain,
Never holding on to their bad feelings long enough to work them through.
They develop a false sense of self with deep shame hidden within
And go into a rage to avoid the vulnerable feelings and remorse.
The person caught in the shame/rage spiral feels bad inside,
Then vents his or her anger to avoid the bad feelings
And then feels bad about blowing up.
"Not-so-nice people" are held hostage by their own shame and bad feelings,
Caught in a sequence of uncomfortable events and emotions they can't break into.
Inside that angry, aloof person frightened of his own vulnerability
Is a little hurt kid who needs authenticity and love.
True strength is found in sharing feelings and being real.
People who can put tears to their vulnerability and pain are called human.

Their best course for those afraid of looking at their feelings might be **From Anger to Hurt and Getting to the Bottom of It All: Real People Can Be Vulnerable and Survive.**

40

What You Think Is What You Are

Heat not a furnace for your foe so hot that it do singe yourself.

—SHAKESPEARE

The amount of mads we have inside depends on what we say to ourselves,
   For Human Beings sometimes are irrational beings,
   Who frequently tell themselves irate, hot thoughts.
   Hot thoughts are negative words that keep us riled up and angry.
   Criticizing and blaming others turn up the heat inside.
   The word anger comes from the Latin word *angere,* meaning "to choke."
   In the heat of high arousal, common sense becomes all choked up.
   The brain turns to mush and the tongue turns acid.
   Irrational thoughts born of anger can do us in.
   The angry enemy inside can be more dangerous than the one outside.

Some Human Beings spend an inordinate amount of time condemning others,
   For Human Beings are judgmental beings
   Flaring up over what others do or don't do
   And playing the game of "Ain't it awful?" about other people's behavior.
   Judgmental people spend time and energy being upset about others
   That they don't have much of a life of their own.
   They are busy figuring out what is morally wrong for other people
   And pointing their "bony finger of blame" at someone else,
   While believing that they are always Mr. or Ms. Right.
   The "bony finger of blame" always hurts both ways—
   The one who is being criticized and the one who points.

Take the first semester course on this topic named **Stop Blaming Others and Focus on Your Own Stuff.** The textbook for the course is **Look at Your Own Self-Angering Thoughts.**

Some Human Beings use their anger to suck others dry,
> For some Human Beings are controlling beings
> Who criticize others constantly to greedily snatch their life energy.
> Negative people pull out a straw and do the "Big Slurp"
> In which their blaming and blaming words of criticism say,
> *"Gimme, gimme, gimme. You must do it my way."*
> Shaming and blaming are destructive forces that invade and depreciate.
> Constant criticism penetrates, tears and rips the other person,
> While it willfully insists on how things must be.
> The "Big Slurp" tactic is of dominance and invasion.

Some submissive Human Beings invite disapproving remarks,
> It is as if they have a complementary inner script of
> *"I'm worthless. Take my energy. I'm unlovable."*
> Overly compliant people have an internal Velcro hook of unworthiness
> That proclaims "I'm no good" and reaches out to meet
> That Velcro fastener of disapproval from the critical partner.
> People who are scolded and belittled contract their energy
> And try to be as invisible as possible saying,
> *"Don't look at me. I'm not here."*
> Human Beings who are criticized often tiptoe around,
> And their energy stops moving and becomes stagnant.

Take a basic physics course on **Energy 101** to understand the "Big Slurp" dynamics.

Habitually angry people are uninformed
    For some Human Beings are ignorant beings
    Who nurse their self-sabotaging beliefs keeping themselves caught in misery.
    They even create anger to keep others from coming close
    And protect themselves from the possibility of being hurt again.
    Hostility, criticism and fault-finding alienate those they love.
    Distrusting people view their world through lenses of suspicion and fear.
    Their paranoia keeps them separate from the rest of the human race
    And their world does turn out to be unfriendly because of their beliefs.
    Or is it that their beliefs are unfriendly?
    Don't think of angry people as bad—
    Just uninformed and separate from knowledge.

The course for feeling-impaired people who are uniformed and uneducated is **Taking Care of Your Feelings in Ways That Do Not Alienate the Rest of the Human Race.**

Advanced Course Work:
What You Can Do with Your Mads

Men are not moved by things but by the views which they take of them.

— EPICTETUS

It is strange where Human Beings put their mads.
Some throw their mads on other people.
Some displace their mads at things like walls.
Some take it out on weaker people.
And some beat themselves up with their mads.
Some refuse to believe that they have any anger.
Others stuff their mads down inside their bodies.
A few Human Beings use their mads to change the world.

Human Beings can made different choices for their angry emotions and behavior:
They can move toward the problem with force (fight).
Move away from the problem (flight).
Hide away from the problem (out of sight).
Or breathe, stay calm, confront and work it out (right).
Fight, flight, out of sight or make it right;
Human Beings are marvelous creatures who have brains wired for choices.

Do you subscribe to the caveman style of fight or flight when angry? Or the medieval practices of blaming others? Then take a modern-day course in **Finding Safe and Sane Ways to Express Your Anger.**

For centuries Human Beings have been trying to control their mads,
   But strong negative emotions are unruly creatures
   That defy and resist being willed or dominated.
   However, the mads can be talked to and reasoned with.
   It's not so much what happened to you;
   It's how you perceive what happened.
   And more important, it is what you do about it.
   As much as we would like, we can't always stop angry feelings,
   However, we can make good decisions about our actions.
   We can't always control angry feelings when they come,
   However we can choose what to do about them.

   Choices. It is about choices.
   Life is about choices.
   Taking one's personal power is about making good choices.
   We don't have to keep doing the same-o, same-o.
   We can learn to choose safe ways to take care of our mads.
   We members of the Great Human Tribe can be very, very choicy
   When it comes to expressing our mads.

To learn more about opening up your life to more options, take the
course **Yes, You Have Choices about Your Unruly Emotions!**

Those mads are the most misunderstood emotion
    For Human Beings who are confused beings who are
    So uncomfortable with angry feelings that they give them a bad rap.
    Most Human Beings are scared of the mads—
    Their own anger and other people's.
    The fear surrounding the unpredictability of anger makes people leery.
    Now anger can be a perfectly splendid emotion.
    After all, it is a necessary part of the survival of the Great Human Tribe.
    Maybe the mads need to hire a new press agent.

Submissive people getting up off their knees may go through an angry stage.
    Anger can be used to help a person leave a bad situation.
    Sometimes anger helps a person separate from their loss
    And define who he or she is apart from other people.
    Doormats can learn to hold on to their anger to protect themselves
    Until they figure out how to negotiate to get their needs met.
    Righteous anger has its place in the history of Human Beings.
    Unlike abusive anger, anger for positive change
    Does not pierce and tear but passes right through others leaving them intact
    With the great cleansing energy of *"It's time for a change.*
    Let's do something different. Let's take corrective action."

    Then the word *mad* can become ***Make A Difference!***

What a different world this would be if everyone would take the course on **Corrective Action: Anger for Positive Change in the World.**

Yes, the mads do have their own place in Human Beings.
  The momentum of anger can be used to accomplish great and lofty tasks.
  People need their mads when their sense of justice has been threatened
  For those who oppress others do not relinquish power easily.
  Necessary revolutions have started with people's anger.
  Collective anger has been used to topple regimes and build new empires.
  Mads can be used as a vehicle for change
  Or to even start one's own personal revolution.

Human Beings no longer need to label anger as always "bad."
  More important is the intention behind the anger
  And the means by which it is used.
  The mads can be a handy thing to have around for special occasions.
  The energy of anger can be used for positive social change.
  Human Beings can learn to confront injustice in whatever form it takes.
  People need to hold on to their mads for when they really need them.
  So never try to take away a person's anger
  Just try to help them understand it and redirect it in beneficial ways.

The proper course to take on how to use your anger in healthy ways is
Righteous Anger and World Change 101.

However, some kinds of anger should never be accepted.
>Like those harmful mads which end up hurting others
>And the destructive effects of anger which invade people's life force.
>Enraged behaviors which violate human rights should not be condoned,
>Nor angry acts which strip others of their dignity.
>We can choose to confront bullying, intimidation and destruction
>And take our power as people to step forward to say
>*"This is wrong. I will stand up and speak out."*
>Cruelty and violence in all their forms should be challenged and opposed.
>We Human Beings can examine our use of dominant, destructive energies.
>Vindictive anger must be stopped for the Great Human Tribe to evolve.

Now it is tricky when people opens up their big cases of the mads
>And start throwing them out on you.
>Angry energy ricochets around the room looking for a place to stick.
>Like Velcro fasteners looking around for hooks in other people,
>Angry energy seeks a bonding site such as hooks or barbs
>Of your own unresolved anger issues waiting to be activated.
>If you have no sticky surface for angry energy to hold onto
>Angry energy can go around you, over you or move right through.

Some Human Beings make wise choices when dealing with other people's mads.
>They don't accept it, don't reflect it and don't reciprocate it.
>They let the anger blow right through like the wind in the willows
>Until it blows itself out of the territory.
>An angry person can easily exhaust himself
>When the other person doesn't take it in or give it back.
>It's hard to blast anger for more than a few minutes
>Without a corresponding receptor site to go into.
>Sometimes, other people's anger hook can be defused
>By just refusing to have a place they can hang it on.

A course to take to learn to deal with other people's flare ups is **No More Button Pushing—Learn to Deactivate Your Anger Hooks.**

Wise Human Beings know that anger fueled by anger makes things worse.
    So therein come those choices that Human Beings get to make.
    At times the thing to do is to just let the other person cool down.
    Sometimes the best action is to escape from angry energy.
    However, at times it is impossible to run away,
    So some Human Beings resort to running away in their minds
    Especially when their feelings of the bads come up.
    Some people leave big time and skip out of their bodies when threatened,
    Leaving to protect themselves from the other person's angry energy.
    Skipping out may help avoid the negative situation temporarily,
    But nobody's home if a person leaves his body.

Running from problems doesn't allow release of internal anger receptors.
    Not having a "say so" stagnates one's personal energy,
    And shuts down the Human Being's personal life force.
    With practice, we can learn to stay present in the face of danger
    And concentrate on the needs at that moment.
    And to breathe. And breathe. And breathe.
    Brain cells need oxygen to help figure things out.
    We can take care of ourselves under conditions of threat
    And put up a shield to keep the negative energy of other people out,
    We can say and do what is needed to problem solve the issue.
    Taking our "say so" is owning our personal power.

So, the course in staying present in the face of anger is called **Be Here Now: Staying Present, Breathing and Dealing Straight from Your Center While Taking Your Say So.**

Human Beings can learn to use firm and fair words when threatened,
   We can speak our anger in safe ways that do not hurt others.
   We can stand up for ourselves by saying what we want.
   We can use strong, fair words instead of using put-downs and fists.
   We can say who we are and state our bottom line.
   One of the best things to do with anger is to tell others how we feel.
   "I messages" are special ways Human Beings get their mads out.
   We can learn to contain our anger in our very own space, remembering
   That our right to get angry ends where other people's bodies begin.

Most of the time it is okay to say how we feel.
   Using our firm and fair words is a way to get the upset feelings out.
   Stating feelings is a caring and healthy thing to do for ourselves
   To keep our angry energy from being stored inside.
   The other person may not care about what we want
   And may laugh it off or put us down for sharing feelings.
   Then we can confront them saying,
   "Hey, don't discount my feelings. I have a right to my feelings."
   We can't expect others to change just because we share angry feelings.
   We can say it how it is and can feel good because we stood up for
   ourselves.
   Other times it's just not necessary or it's dangerous to say how we feel.
   We can choose whether to say what is going on feeling-wise or not.
   The right to take one's say-so is a prerogative of being a Human Being.

You guessed it. The public speaking course to take here is **Taking My Power: I Say What I Mean and I Mean What I Say.**

A field study course in sharing uncomfortable feelings might be **Maybe I'll Say My Feelings and Maybe I Won't; Sometimes I Do and Sometimes I Don't.**

DEEP BREATHS

FIRM & FAIR WORDS

I-MESSAGES

REMINDERS TO COOL DOWN

STICK TO ONE ISSUE

LISTENING

TIME OUTS TO COOL DOWN

Some people are learning how to fight fair,
    For Human Beings are evolving beings
    Who use fair fighting as a vehicle for change and self-definition.
    Fair fighting says,
    "Take your power instead of going into helplessness or rage.
    Fight consciously. Observe what you are doing. Be awake.
    Don't turn it all over to that robot who lives on automatic pilot
    And responds angrily out of hurt and the desire to prove one's point.
    Respect yourself and the other person,
    Feel good about the process of disagreement rather than trying to win."

Clearly spoken, angry feelings can be the challenge to say:
    "This is what I stand for: / This is my bottom line.
    This is what I want. / This is who I am.
    See me for who I am.

    And tell me, what you stand for? / What do you want?
    Tell me of your bottom line.
    I care about who you are, just as I care about me.
    I am willing to see you for who you are."

    "I can be me. You can be you. / We can agree to disagree. We can work it out
    And continue to be loving with each other."

Fair fighting techniques are taught in the workshops on **Conscious Loving and Conscious Fighting.**

How novel these tools of fighting fair are.
   Being responsible for one's own thoughts, feelings and behavior,
   Learning about one's own hidden agendas for control and power,
   And negotiating and compromising instead of blaming and shaming.
   Human Beings can practice the fine art of respecting each other
   Even in times of intense disagreement.
   Now fair fighting is not an easy task,
   But such a challenging and noble one.
   Some people choose to use the tools of fair fighting
   Acting constructively with their anger
   Even when the other person does not.
   Respectful negotiation and the ability to soothe each other
   After a blowup are the major keys to achieving a happy relationship.
   Equality between people puts a premium on bargaining everything.
   We Human Beings are as mentally healthy as we are able
   To take responsibility for our own thoughts and behaviors.

- **CHILL OUT WORDS**
- LET IT GO
- IT'S NOT IMPORTANT
- OH WELL...
- DON'T SWEAT THE SMALL STUFF
- TAKE A CHILL PILL

Why not go for your Black Belt in **Above the Belt Assertive Training for the Formerly Weak and Puny?**

Being able to laugh at one's self does wonders to put those mads into perspective.

For Human Beings are also humorous beings,
Who use laughter to heal old hurts and present injustices,
And the body ailments that holding onto anger brings.
True courage is being able to laugh at one's own shortcomings
And live all of life as the receiver of the great Cosmic Joke.
The Cosmic Joke is the universe's way of always saying *"Surprise!*
Hellooo! Are you getting this yet?
Quit taking yourself so seriously.
Here are the surprises we have lined up for you to deal with today.
You can choose what to do with your mads. "
The Cosmic Joke's secret punch line is
"Surrender yourself to the Divine Comedy of Life."

For help here, get yourself down to the local comedy club and sign up for sessions on **Taking Yourself Lightly.**

One of the Marvelous Things about Being a Human Being Is to Learn to Observe Uncomfortable Feelings.

We are healed of great suffering only by experiencing it to the full.
— MARCEL PROUST

Human Beings can be very creative in finding ways to hang onto their anger
    For Human Beings are resistant beings
    Who often deny that they have a problem with their mads.
    Denial has many voices that proclaim the energy of being stuck:
    "I don't have a problem.
    I have a problem, but it's not important.
    I have an important problem, but it will go away soon.
    I have an important problem that won't go away, but I can't ask for help.
    I have an important problem that won't go away. I need help, but it's
    hopeless."
    There is a vast reservoir of pride and fear beneath resistance to change.
    Going through the fear barrier is necessary for those who want to be free.
    Riding the mood swing roller coaster of highs and lows
    The emotions that anger covers up must be fully explored.
    Hurt, fear, shame and emptiness wait for their human to focus within.

At times in a Human Being's life, denial no longer works.
　　And the frozen feelings that loom down in the depths start to thaw.
　　Those disagreeable emotions seek to be acknowledged.
　　Confusion asks for airing out in the light of day.
　　Numbness may be ready to take a big stretch and open up.
　　The hurt and pain of betrayal long for understanding.
　　The fear hiding beneath the anger aches to be explored.
　　The "should monster" keeps rearing its ugly head.
　　Persistent, unregulated anger may be a sign that
　　The Human Being's frozen feelings and beliefs need defrosting.

Try the course **Observation and Coping 498: A Practicum in Advanced Living—From Anger to Empowerment.**

The forms that the negative human emotions take are varied and wide
  And are shaped strongly by your choices of thoughts and words.
  Observation of your words both inner and outer is part of the course
  work.
  Investigation of your internal landscape is the first step to understanding.
  Human Beings who are angry can learn to simply observe their emotions
  And develop a part of themselves called the "Silent Observer."
  The "Silent Observer" is neutral about what's going on emotion-wise.
  It is "The One Who Watches" who just collects data.
  Angry and hurt feelings can be observed. Not judged.
  Just watched and experienced. Nor run away from. Nor made bad.
  Anger can be felt and called by name as such.
  "Well, would you look at this. I'm feeling hot-headed. I'm mad.
  I'll sit with it for a while. What is this about for me?
  What is underneath here? Hmmm."
  Uncomfortable feelings are simply an invitation for their human to
  look further.

HE'S STARTING
TO GET
STEAMED...
HIS STOMACH
IS STARTING
TO CHURN...
NOW HIS
FIST IS
STARTING
TO CLENCH...
HE'S TELLING
HIMSELF,
"THIS ISN'T
FAIR!"

Our "Silent Observer" within patiently sits and waits,
    Amusedly noting the comings and goings of feelings,
    And taking in the ride of the ups and downs of the emotional roller coaster.
    Observing the fear energy in its many disguises:
    The angers, the jealousies, the pettiness, the frustrations,
    And the attachments, addictions and the need to be in control.
    Watching the thoughts, feelings, tension and reactions.
    The "Silent Observer" watches as fear steps forward into the foreground.
    Fear of failure, fear of success, fear of closeness,
    Fear of abandonment and loss. Fear of death.
    And perhaps the greatest fear of all:
    Fear of intense feelings and being out of control
    Fear is not necessarily bad.
    It is only the little kid dressed up in a scary monster suit.
    Creating the very same monster it wishes to get rid of.

Watching, our Silent Observer nods its head without judgment.
    When viewed in the proper light, fear can be seen for what it is—
    Fear is only an illusion to be experienced and understood.
    Our power as strong and free individuals begins where our fear ends.
    At some point in life, the roller coaster ups and downs grow tedious.
    The little kid begins to take off the monster suit,
    And gets off the roller coaster,
    And heads for the merry-go-round
    To grab the brass ring and get on with life.

To enroll in this advanced technique of balancing the emotions, take the course called **Zen and the Art of Mindfulness.**

The Dark Side

You don't know how much power the dark side has.

— DARTH VADAR

All Human Beings have a dark side that they have trouble facing.
>For Human Beings are also shadowy beings
>Who hide their dark parts and secret fears about being bad in their
>backpack.
>The dark is the unruly stepchild of chaos.
>It is the stuff of the shadow lurking in the background.
>It's the ferment of swirling energy of shame.
>Denial of the shadow part helps people avoid looking within
>To see their own dirty laundry hidden away in all that baggage.

Traits of the dark side can be traced back through the generations.
>The dirty laundry of unfinished business hides in the closet.
>What we dislike about ourselves, we can't stand in others.
>We criticize and blame others when we can't accept our own behavior.
>If our parents had a negative character flaw
>We can't stand that same behavior in others
>Even though it may be a secret part of ourselves.
>And yet, we may be attracted to a person who has same traits
>Or end up with a boss who has those same irritating ways
>Or worse yet, even marry someone with similar ways of acting.
>The dark side says *"You spot it, you got it!*
>*Let's deal with what you don't like about yourself,*
>*Or you will repeat that same lesson until you work it through."*

The dark side can be a powerful ally when used for growth and evolution.
>The dark is not necessarily bad.
>Its fear base is merely lack of understanding.
>The shadow side is that part of us that longs for self-growth
>While being terrified of it at the same time.
>The dark is that which seeks the light.
>Remember the little kid dressed in his monster suit?
>The dark side provides triple insurance to get its stuff worked through.

The lab course for dealing with the dark side is **Spring Housecleaning: Airing Out the Dirty Linen**.

60

At times in a Human Being's life, come great fits of mads and bads.

> Life begins to fall apart in rapid order.
> Chaos erupts with wildly swinging emotions.
> Crisis in a person's life is a wake-up call, saying,
> *"Wake up. Wake up. It's time to go to class!*
> *Get busy on your homework.*
> *Your old ways of doing things don't work anymore.*
> *Your robot is running out of batteries.*
> *It's time to do something different.*
> *Wake up! Look at the contents of your backpack and suitcase.*
> *Don't go back to sleep!"*

Then the dark side must be acknowledged and honored for what it is:

> Part and parcel of the human experience.
> The energy of the chaos can be used to address those necessary lessons
> And open up what has been hidden away.
> Deep, dark secrets of a lifetime can be brought forth
> And called by name for what they are:
> Neglect. Abuse. Loss. Grief. Pain. Fear. Emptiness.
> The depth of the emotions can bring the person to his knees.
> The cry for release goes out, *"Help me! I surrender.*
> *I can no longer carry this heavy baggage by myself."*

Sorry—very few courses are taught on how to surrender. **This high level skill can best be examined by meditation, seeking out a self-help group or going into therapy.**

Then the soul bids the person to seek the help of other loving Human Beings.

Spirit comes forth to assist in the journey
For Human Beings are also heavenly beings
Who use crisis to shake out the contents of their backpack and suitcase.
The energy of chaos brings the dirty laundry to the light of day
To get turned out for a rigorous scrubbing.
Then, when all seems darkest, shift happens.
Human Beings have this miraculous ability to make shift happen.
Perhaps, in the long run, everyone gets to experience everything.
That's one of the marvelous things about being a Human Being.

Across a lifetime of many times of anger turned inward or outward,
  Some people mellow out, learning that they don't have to be perfect.
  They learn to chill down their self-angering hot thoughts.
  They use affirming words to address the negative messages.
  They stop their "shoulds, oughts, musts and have-tos."
  Their "should monster" is given a gold watch and retired.
  Tickets are on sale for "That Great Journey of Life called Self-Acceptance."
  Human Beings can step forward and purchase their tickets at any time,
  Courageously walking through the areas of hurt and betrayal,
  Though the regions of pain, fear and emptiness,
  By watching, simply watching.
  With each mistake along the way and the commitment to change,
  Human Beings can learn to empty out their mads baggage.

The course to take here on airing the emotions is **The Past Doesn't Matter Anymore: Getting It All Out, Then Letting It All Go.**

It is a sad but true fact that Human Beings must use pain to wake up,
For Human Beings are dense beings,
Who must hit bottom to break into denial.
Wake-up calls are necessary for Human Beings to become truly alive
And shake up that sleep-walking robot who goes woodenly
Through the motions of this, The Great Drama of Life.

Warning:
If you don't get it right, then you are in for another round of pain.

Warning:
Don't hit the snooze button on your wake-up call!

The how-to-course to take for waking up is **Giving Up the Robot and Becoming a Real Human Being.**

Yes, You Can Transform Your Mads

Step out of your cave; the world awaits you like a garden.

— NIETZSCHE

Some preach that we should forgive those with whom we are angry.
   Now forgiveness is necessary to get to be a grown-up Human Being.
   Forgiveness is "The Big Let Go."
   Releasing the need to judge and condemn others helps clear out the mads.
   Forgiving others to obtain peace of mind is only one half of the picture.
   Forgiving ourselves for our shortcomings is the other part.
   But forgiveness can never be imposed by self or others as a "should."
   Willing ourselves to forgive does not make anger automatically go away.
   Forgiveness does not happen just because others say we should.
   Mads, being cantankerous creatures, just do not work that way.
   Remember, the human condition is to have strong, crabby emotions—
   And those backpacks and suitcases to carry them around in,
   Containing all sorts of mads at ourselves and others,
   And all those bads because we are not who we think we should be.
   And choices.
   Choices of what we are going to do about them.

There are no courses taught on forgiveness. To better understand this profoundly deep shift of consciousness, try getting down on your knees and praying.

Hope springs eternal within our backpacks and suitcases.
    Hope, like that which lay hidden at the bottom of Pandora's box
    When she loosed the plagues and sorrows upon the world.
    Fortunately underneath all of our mads and bads,
    Hope stirs within each Human Being who longs for peace.
    For some people, the buried hurt, anger and rage needs must be vented
    Then, at times with great grace,
    Forgiveness comes of its own accord.
    Surrendering to the call from the soul,
    Compassion and love take the place of the hurt underneath the anger.

For instructions on course work on Beingness, **check in with your Higher Power.**

Self-acceptance of anger and other negative human traits has great advantages:

> Your central nervous system and vital parts let go of the overload.
> You give up wearing yourself out trying to get others to change.
> You take yourself lightly and have tons of energy left over for creativity.
> You treat all living things including yourself with respect.
> Your robot is retired to the attic into permanent storage.
> You feel empowered standing up for yourself.
> Laughter erupts often from triumph over hardship and pain.
> The stuff of life becomes precious:
> Like honesty, integrity, and a sense of the ridiculous,
> And you start writing jokes for your Great Cosmic Jokebook.

Difficult lessons are presented near the end of Human Being's life.

> That final exam is a doozy with belief-busting questions:
> *What judgments and prejudices did you let go?*
> *What amends did you make to those you have injured*
> *What is undone? What is unfinished?*
> *Did you ever retire that should monster?*
> *Whatever happened to that dirty linen?*
> *In spite of all the pain and trauma, did you learn to laugh at yourself?*
> *Did you ever get the Cosmic Joke?*
> *What do you still long for within your heart of hearts?*
> *And most important, what is the quality of your loving?*

People who have learned to contain their anger, express it appropriately and release it safely have completed a major part of the lessons: **The Final Course: Living Life Passionately and Eloquently.**

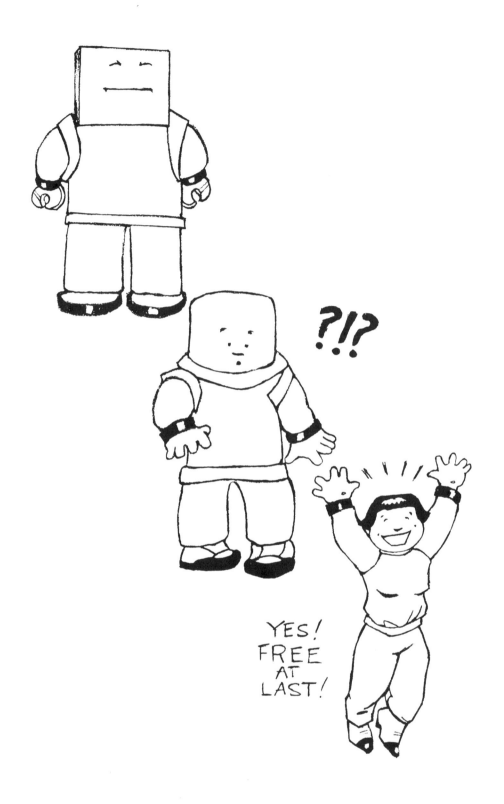

Marvelous things begin to happen as you move through the mads curriculum
Assigned to you as a member of the Great Human Tribe
And let go of the contents of that backpack and suitcase.
Please understand that you need not get rid of your anger,
But you can move it to a higher place where it can be carefully used.
Yes, your mads are a wonderful but exacting teacher in the Great
School of Life.
Emotions must be experienced and expressed so you can evolve.
Feeling is healing.
When you share your feelings openly and sincerely, you are real.
Understanding and compassion are what your mads ask of you.
Love and acceptance of yourself with all your human traits is the goal.
You can learn to stop being an "anger inner" or an "anger outer,"
And become a "safe anger expresser."
You can use your mads to change your world!

Oh, those pesky mads are your teacher all right,
For Human Beings are educable beings
Who can use their mads for personal evolution and growth.
The mads ask you to create new ways of thinking and acting
And invite you to open up new options,
And laugh at yourself for being oh-so-human.
Your mads challenge you to play out new realities.
Novel experiences beyond your wildest dreams await you,
And you get to be a real grown-up Human Being.

LETTING
GO

GRUDGES

ANGERS

OLD
HURTS

RESENTMENTS
ENTITLEMENT

Life is full of multidimensional possibilities,
    For Human Beings are evolutional beings,
    Whose future has many possible outcomes.
    Once you get a handle on the mads course work,
    Your life becomes easier and easier.
    Remember, you don't have to keep on doing the same-o, same-o.

    Choices.
    Life is about choices.
    The Great Human Drama is all about choices.
    One great thing about being a Human Being is that we do get choices.
    We can graduate this School of Life with honors.
    We can use our choices about our mads to become gentle, loving people.

    What better option do you have to do with your lifetime?
    Choose wisely.

Helper Words for Human Beings to Take Care of Their Anger

I am in charge of my own feelings.
    I own my feelings.
    I feel them, name them and then tell them.
    It is okay to feel angry.
    I learn how to express my anger in ways that are helpful.

I am in charge of my own behavior.
    I may not be able to control my anger, but I have choices what I do with it.
    I make good choices over how I let my anger out.
    I watch my thoughts. Hot thoughts keep me angry.
    Cool thoughts calm me.
    I practice cooling off. I learn to chill myself out. I take a mental chill pill.
    I feel good about being responsible for chilling myself out.

I remember people are precious. I am precious.
    I stop hurting others or myself with my anger.
    I watch my thoughts. I watch my words. I watch my actions.
    I own the hurtful words and actions that I do to others.
    I learn about things I do when I am stressed and threatened.
    I stop hurting people with my words and actions.
    I feel good about treating people with kindness.

I choose to feel good about myself through speaking out.
    I express angry feelings in ways that are fair to others and myself.
    I use my firm and fair words: "I feel ____ when you ____."
    I tell my feelings and then try to work things out.
    I feel good about saying what I feel and what I stand for.

I don't have to hold on to my anger.
    I find ways to let my anger go.
    I talk about my hurt feeling and angry feelings.
    I problem solve things that make me upset.
    I keep looking until I find someone safe to talk to about my anger.
    I talk about my words and actions that hurt others.

I take my power!
    I stand up for myself. I stand up for others who are being hurt.
    I interrupt my mean thoughts that I use to beat myself up.
    I feel good about learning about myself.
    I am powerful when I use my fair and firm words.

Sharing Feelings: Staying Safe by Speaking Straight

S.	Share feelings.	Stay in the present by owning your own feelings during conflict. Breathe deep to center yourself. Use the "I formula": "I feel _____ when you _____." State the behavior of the other person that upsets you. State what you would like to have happen. "What I would like you to do is _____." Remember, we do not always get what we want. Observe your personal reaction as you take this risk.
A.	Accept feelings.	Validate your right to have your feelings. Say how you feel. Acknowledge the other person's right to have their feelings. Breathe deeply and stay centered when feeling threatened.
	Avoid blame.	Observe yourself closely for the use of "You Messages" which put down, label, criticize, judge or threaten the other person. Counter discounting of your feelings by stating you have the right to own your feelings. Say, "I feel _____ when you do not listen to my feelings." Confront blaming "You messages." "I will not allow you to call me names. Let's stick to the problem here."
F.	Find out facts.	Sort out fact from fiction. Check out your interpretations and assumptions of the situation. Look at your need to control.
	Focus on the issue, not personalities.	Look at your need to be right. Stay on track. Focus specifically on what is important to you. Say what you want.
	Focus on positive outcomes.	Take time out if you get too heated or overwhelmed. Sort out feelings and facts. Keep emphasizing that the two of you can work it out. Brainstorm compromises and other ideas. Risk!

E.	Empty yourself of the need to be right.	Focus on your responsibility to look after yourself instead of trying to defend yourself against accusations. Watch your anxious need to fix, convert, protect, distract or submit. Determine if these ways of coping with threat make you happy. Practice the fine art of surrendering your rigid need to be in control. Ask yourself, "Do I want to be right or be happy?" Laugh at your rigid control thoughts which keep you stuck.
	Encourage yourself and the other person.	Give acknowledgments and appreciations. Say how you would like the problem to be worked through. Go to problem solving and stay there. Ask how you both can take care of each other in this situation. Stay task oriented by seeking solutions to your mads. Make love instead of war.

Dialogue with the Mads in Each Other

"In the end, dear, all that matters is the loving."
— ELIZABETH GOUDGE'S FATHER ON HIS DEATHBED

Look into your partner's eyes as you place one hand on their heart and your other hand over their hand on your heart. Go through several rounds of saying each phase to each other.

I honor the hurt and wounded child in you as I ask you to honor the hurt and wounded child in me.

I see you for who you are, a hurt and wounded child, who seeks love by _____ as I too am a hurt and wounded child.

My interest is to make love instead of war, but my hurt and wounded child needs to say, _____.

When I feel hurt and wounded, I use the angry behavior of (criticizing, controlling, blaming, shaming, withdrawal) and I ask you to see my angry behavior as evidence of my wounds.

I thank your for openness about _____, that allows me feel be safe to _____.

I honor your vulnerability as you talk about _____ and I ask you to honor my vulnerability when I talk about _____.

At this moment, what I offer to you is _____. What I would like from you is _____.

I thank you for choosing me to learn your great lessons of _____ as I learn my great lessons of _____.

I see you for who you are, a strong and independent individual, who and I too am a strong and independent individual.

In the end dear, all that matters is the loving.

Acknowledgments

My teacher, Virginia Satir, one of the co-founders of family therapy, first described the concepts of *The Bony Finger of Blame, The Settle Down Buttons,* and *The Big Game of Life.* The exercise Sharing Feelings: Staying Safe by Speaking Straight is based on a conflict negotiation model described by Scott Peck in *The Different Drum.* The concepts of the different levels of denial are attributed to psychologist Ken Moses.

Special credit goes to Suzanne Schinkel, who help me conceptualize the energetics of anger.

Thanks go to the following people who thoughtfully contributed phrases to the text: John Grimes, Marcia White, Marilyn Miller, John Freedom, Jean Hogan, Les Brown, Kathi Buchholtz, Colleen Lansdale, Donna Gilson, Thom Cooper, and Nancy Sarama. Thanks also go to those dedicated researchers and psychologists in anger theory who have contributed to our current knowledge about this hot topic.

Harrison Shaffer of Whitewing Press in San Francisco provided technical assistance in bringing this book to press.

About the Author

Lynne Namka is one of those nice people who has to keep on examining her own mad baggage. She wonders why she has written two books on anger and founded a toy company, Talk, Trust and Feel Therapeutics, which provides curriculums and products for angry children. Lynne is a psychologist in private practice in Tucson, Arizona. She lives with her husband and cat, Dené, at the base of the Santa Catalina mountains and has a full time job learning to be a real Human Being.

Therapists and teachers may request a catalog from *Talk, Trust and Feel Therapeutics* by sending a SASE. Further copies of *How to Let Go of Your Mad Baggage* and *The Mad Family Gets Their Mads Out: Fifty Things Your Family Can Say and Do to Express Anger Constructively* can be ordered from Talk, Trust and Feel Therapeutics, 5398 Golder Ranch Road, Tucson, Arizona 85739 for $12.95 (each) ppd. or $22.95 ppd. for both books. Our e-mail address is "harnack@rtd.com."

If we are to reach real peace in the world, we shall have to begin with the children.

—GANDHI

Also by Lynne Namka

"A TOTAL CROCK!"

THE MAD FAMILY
GETS THEIR
MADS OUT

LYNNE NAMKA

← EXPERT CRITIC

AT BOOKSTORES
EVERYWHERE
or

$12.95 postpaid

from:
TALK, TRUST & FEEL
THERAPEUTICS
5398 Golder Ranch Road
Tucson, AZ 85739

E-mail: harnack@rtd.com